Pebble®

Out in Space

The Moon

by Martha E. H. Rustad

Consulting Editor: Gail Saunders-Smith, PhD

Consultant: Roger D. Launius, PhD
Senior Curator, Division of Space History
National Air and Space Museum
Smithsonian Institution, Washington, D.C.

Capstone
press®

Mankato, Minnesota

Pebble Books are published by Capstone Press,
151 Good Counsel Drive, P.O. Box 669, Mankato, Minnesota 56002.
www.capstonepress.com

1 2 3 4 5 6 13 12 11 10 09 08

Library of Congress Cataloging-in-Publication Data
Rustad, Martha E. H. (Martha Elizabeth Hillman), 1975–
    The moon / by Martha E. H. Rustad. — Rev. and updated.
    p. cm. — (Pebble Books. Out in space)
    Summary: "Photographs and simple text introduce the features of the Moon,
Earth's only natural satellite" — Provided by publisher.
    Includes bibliographical references and index.
    ISBN-13: 978-1-4296-1718-5 (hardcover)
    ISBN-10: 1-4296-1718-7 (hardcover)
    ISBN-13: 978-1-4296-2811-2 (softcover)
    ISBN-10: 1-4296-2811-1 (softcover)
    1. Moon — Juvenile literature. I. Title.
QB582.R87 2009
523.3 — dc22   2007051336

Note to Parents and Teachers

The Out in Space set provides the most up-to-date solar system
information to support national science standards. This book
describes and illustrates the Moon. The photographs support early
readers in understanding the text. This book also introduces early
readers to subject-specific vocabulary words, which are defined
in the Glossary section. Early readers may need assistance to read
some words and to use the Table of Contents, Glossary, Read More,
Internet Sites, and Index sections of the book.

Table of Contents

A Shining Light 5

What Is the Moon? 13

The Moon's Surface 19

Glossary 22

Read More 23

Internet Sites. 23

Index 24

A Shining Light

The Moon shines
high above Earth.
It brightens
the night sky.

The Moon is easy
to find at night.
Sometimes you can see
the Moon during the day.

Moon

Sun

Earth

The Moon reflects
the Sun's light to Earth.
The sunlit part of the
Moon seems to glow.

Sometimes only part
of the sunlit side
of the Moon faces Earth.
Our view makes it seem like
the Moon changes shape.

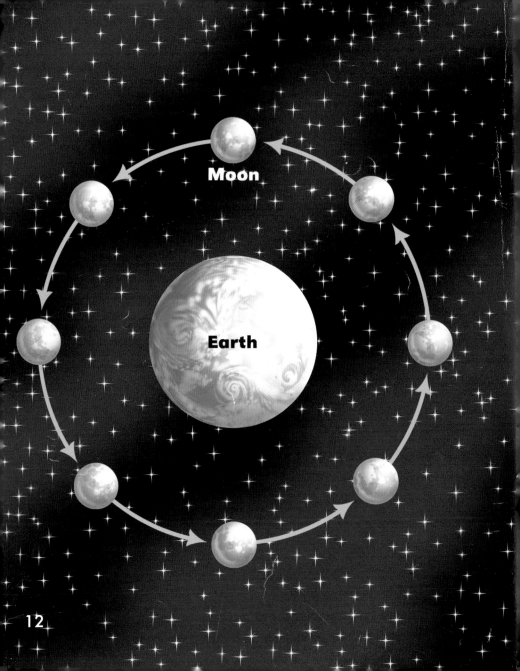

What Is the Moon?

The Moon is Earth's satellite.
It moves around Earth
once every 28 days.
The same side of the Moon
always faces Earth.

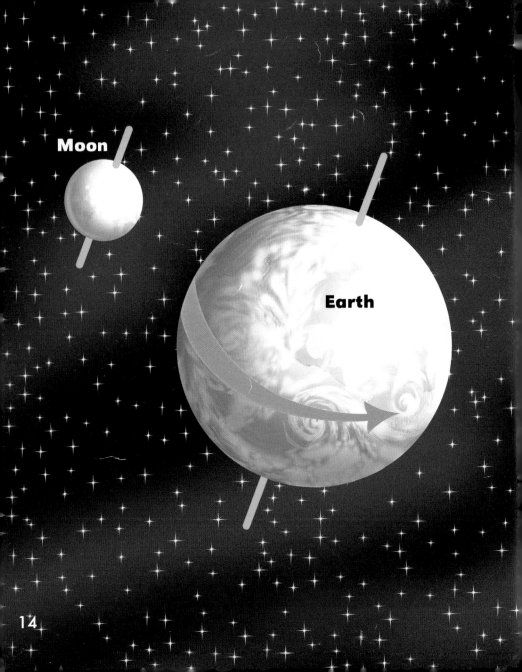

Moon

Earth

14

Earth spins once each day.
The Moon looks like
it moves from east
to west as Earth spins.

Earth

Moon

The Moon is much
smaller than Earth.
About 50 Moons
could fit inside Earth.

The Moon's Surface

Craters dot the Moon.
These holes make the
Moon's surface rough.

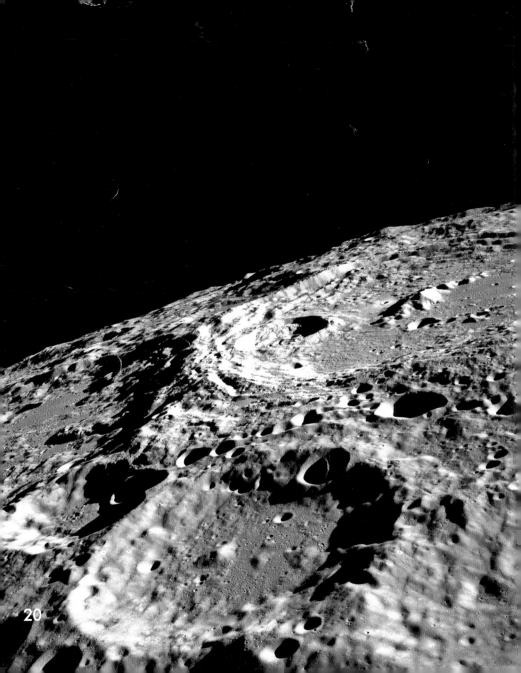

20

The Moon is not like Earth.
Gray dust and rocks
cover the Moon.
The sky is always black.

Glossary

crater — a hole made when objects crash into a planet's or moon's surface

Earth — the planet we live on

glow — to give off a low, even light

reflect — to return light from an object; the Moon reflects light from the Sun.

satellite — an object that travels around another object in space; the Moon is Earth's satellite.

Sun — the star that the planets and dwarf planets move around; the Sun provides light and heat to the planets and dwarf planets.

surface — the outside or outermost area of something

Read More

Adamson, Thomas K. *The Moon.* Exploring the Galaxy. Mankato, Minn.: Capstone Press, 2007.

Bredeson, Carmen. *What Is the Moon?* I Like Space! Berkeley Heights, N.J.: Enslow, 2008.

Rau, Dana Meachen. *Night Light: A Book about the Moon.* Amazing Science. Minneapolis: Picture Window Books, 2006.

Internet Sites

FactHound offers a safe, fun way to find Internet sites related to this book. All of the sites on FactHound have been researched by our staff.

Here's how:

1. Visit *www.facthound.com*

2. Choose your grade level.

3. Type in this book ID **1429617187** for age-appropriate sites. You may also browse subjects by clicking on letters, or by clicking on pictures and words.

4. Click on the **Fetch It** button.

FactHound will fetch the best sites for you!

Index

craters, 19
day, 7
dust, 21
Earth, 5, 9, 11, 13,
    15, 17, 21
east, 15
glowing, 9
light, 9

night, 5, 7
rocks, 21
satellite, 13
shape, 11
size, 17
Sun, 9
surface, 19
west, 15

Word Count: 150
Grade: 1
Early-Intervention Level: 15

Editorial Credits
Katy Kudela, revised edition editor; Kim Brown, designer and illustrator;
    Jo Miller, photo researcher

Photo Credits
NASA/JSC, 20; NSSDC, 18; Shutterstock/Charlie Bishop, cover, 1;
Shutterstock/Kivrins Anatolijs, 6; Shutterstock/Rafael Pacheco, 10;
Shutterstock/Ruta Saulyte-Laurinaviciene, 4